Hide-and-Seek Science

Animal Camouflage

EMMA STEVENSON

Holiday House / New York

For Gary
My soul mate

HOLIDAY HOUSE is registered in the U.S. Patent and Trademark Office.

Printed and Bound in April 2013 at Tien Wah Press, Johor Bahru, Johor, Malaysia.

The text typeface is Breughel Regular.

The artwork was created with gouache.

www.holidayhouse.com

First Edition

1 3 5 7 9 10 8 6 4 2

Library of Congress Cataloging-in-Publication Data

Stevenson, Emma.

Hide-and-seek science : animal camouflage / Emma Stevenson. — 1st ed.

p. cm.

ISBN 978-0-8234-2293-7 (hardcover)

1. Camouflage (Biology)—Juvenile literature.

I. Title.

QL767.S743 2013

591.47'2—dc23

2011042109

Do you like playing hide-and-seek?
For animals, it isn't just a game.
It's a matter of life and death.
Animals need to hide from predators
that want to eat them!
Predators need to hide so their prey
don't see them and run away.
Animals that have colors and
patterns that match their
environments can be almost
invisible to the eye.
That's called camouflage.
There are 293 animals hidden
in the habitats in this book.
Can you find them?

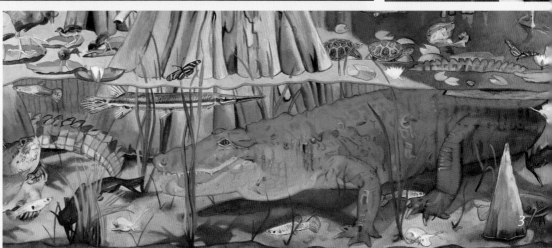

Hide-and-Seek in the Swamp

Can you find 36 animals?

Swamps

Swamps are very wet areas. Some swamps are underwater all year long. Others are covered with water for only part of the year. One of the largest swamps in the world is in southern Florida. It is called the Everglades. Some animals live under the water and some live at the surface of the water. Other animals live above the water or in surrounding areas.

Animals of the Everglades

Alligator: 1–4 Since alligators' eyes and nostrils are high on their heads, they can hide the rest of their bodies underwater.

American green tree frog: 33, 34 These frogs are brown, green, or both brown and green, so they can hide on tree leaves and bark.

Anhinga: 5 These birds can swim while mostly hidden underwater. They are called snake-birds because, with only their long necks sticking up, they look like snakes.

Apple snail: 6–9 Apple snails hide underwater from birds such as the snail kite.

Black-crowned night heron: 10 These herons hunt at dawn and dusk, when their black caps and gray wings make them hard to see.

Catfish: 11–13 Catfish feed on the bottom, where they can blend in with the mud.

Cottonmouth moccasin: 14 Cottonmouths sometimes sunbathe on tree limbs over the water, where they can look like branches.

Diamondback terrapin: 15, 16 The dark backs of diamondback

terrapins look like rocks while they bask in the sun.

Gar: 17 Gars are fish that often float near the surface, where they look like pieces of wood or dead vegetation.

Great egret: 18, 19 Great egrets make nests of sticks in trees or

shrubs, and then hide them with green plants.

Manatee: 20 The gray skin of manatees helps them blend in with the dark swamp.

Mosquito fish: 21–24 These small fish often hide among underwater plants.

Purple gallinule (adult) 25; (chicks) 26–28: Although adult purple gallinules are brightly colored, the chicks are first black and then turn tan to blend in with the swamp.

Raccoon: 29 Raccoons are nocturnal, which means they come out only at night, when their dark markings make them hard to see.

River otter: 30 River otters have brown and gray coats that blend in with water and weeds.

Snail kite: 31 The sooty-gray feathers of these birds of prey look like tree bark.

Snapping turtle: 32 Snapping turtles hide at the bottom of the swamp, covered in mud.

Zebra longwing butterfly: 35, 36 The yellow stripes on these butterflies make it hard to tell whether they are coming or going.

Hide-and-Seek in the Desert

Can you find 34 animals?

Deserts

Deserts are areas that get very little rain. Few plants grow in deserts, because there is not enough water. The biggest hot desert in the world is the Sahara in North Africa. It is hard for desert animals to find water, food, and shelter. They must also protect themselves from the heat. Many dig burrows or hide under the sand and then come out only at night, when it is cooler.

Animals of the Sahara

Camel: 1–10 Camels are sand colored to match the desert.

Cape hare: 11 These mammals come out at night, when their brownish-gray coats can blend in with the darkness.

Desert agama: 12–14 The sandy, gray-brown coloring of these lizards allows them to disguise themselves as rocks.

Desert eagle owl: 15, 16 Desert eagle owls, also called pharaoh eagle owls, have brown and tan feathers that blend in with rocks and sand. They are silent fliers, which lets them sneak up on prey.

Desert hedgehog: 17 The desert hedgehog is one of the smallest hedgehogs. When it is in trouble, it rolls up into a tiny brown ball covered with spines.

Desert monitor lizard: 28 The brown-and-yellow-mottled desert monitor lizards are the largest reptiles in the Sahara.

Dorcas gazelle (adult) 18–20; (fawn) 21: Like most desert

animals, gazelles are born sandy colored.

Fennec: 22 Fennecs are foxes with huge ears and excellent hearing. Their tan coats help them hide in the sand.

Gerbil: 23, 24 Gerbils were originally known as desert rats until they were introduced into North America as pets. Their brown fur blends in with the desert.

Jerboa: 25–27 Jerboas are rodents that look like mini-kangaroos. They hide in burrows that they dig in the desert and come out only at night.

Sand cat: 29 The sand cat's pale fur with black bars makes it hard to see at night, when it comes out.

Sand viper: 30, 31 These snakes hide under the sand with only their eyes and nostrils sticking out.

Scorpion: 32–34 Sand-colored scorpions eat insects and small rodents. They are hard to see in the sand, where they wait to sting their prey with the tips of their tails.

Hide-and-Seek in the Rain Forest

Can you find 33 animals?

Rain Forests

Rain forests have tall trees and get lots of rain. The largest rain forest in the world is the Amazon forest in South America. It is home to some of the world's most unusual animals. While some animals live on the ground, most live in the trees. Many spend their whole lives high above the forest floor.

Animals of the Amazon Rain Forest

Agouti: 1 Agoutis are mammals that are related to guinea pigs. Their brown coats match the rain-forest floor where they live.

Blue morpho butterfly: 4, 5 When a predator passes by, the brilliantly colored blue morpho flashes its bright wings, blinding and confusing the enemy. The underside of the blue morpho's wings is a dull brown, providing camouflage when its wings are closed.

Emerald tree boa: 6, 7 Emerald tree boas are bright green, like the leaves on the trees where they spend their lives.

Giant anteater: 8 The giant anteater is covered with stiff, straw-like gray or brown hair that blends in with the forest floor.

Golden lion tamarin: 9, 10 From a distance, this small monkey's silky, golden-red fur looks like rays of sunlight and brightly colored fruits.

Hummingbird: 11, 12 Hummingbirds are often as brightly colored as the flowers that they visit looking for nectar.

Jaguar: 13 The jaguar is the largest wild cat in South America. It has spots that help it hide in shadows.

Katydid: 14, 15 These insects could be mistaken for leaves.

Leaf toad: 16, 17 Leaf toads live among the litter on the forest floor and look just like leaves.

spots help them hide in the mottled shadows of the rain-forest floor.

Owl butterfly: 20, 21 Owl butterflies have large, eye-shaped spots on their wings that make them look like owls when they are resting.

Poison dart frogs: 22–25 Instead of hiding, these poisonous frogs advertise themselves with bright colors. Most animals know they are poisonous.

Silky anteater: 27 These small anteaters have gold-and-gray fur that blends in with rain-forest trees.

Squirrel monkey: 28, 29 Squirrel monkeys have yellow-and-olive-colored coats that blend in with the rain-forest trees.

Three-toed sloth: 30, 31 Sloths let green algae grow on their fur so they can hide among the leaves.

Toucan: 32, 33 From far away, the toucan's colorful beak makes it look like a fruit instead of a bird.

Macaw (blue and gold 2, 3; scarlet 26): Although macaws are brightly colored, they are actually difficult to spot up in the tree canopy against the golden shafts of sunlight and blue sky. This camouflage gives them protection from large mammals, snakes, and birds of prey.

Monkey frog: 18 These frogs have long limbs and no webbing between their toes, which allows them to hold branches and climb trees just like a monkey. Their patterned skin helps them hide in the trees.

Ocelot: 19 Ocelots are wild cats whose

Hide-and-Seek in the Savanna

Can you find 40 animals?

Savannas

Savannas are big, open spaces of grass with scattered shrubs and trees. There is not enough rain for many trees to grow. Some well-known animals live in the East African savannas. Many are herbivores, or plant-eating animals, that move around in search of grasses and leaves. Meat-eating animals often follow them. In the savannas, animals have to outsmart their enemies to survive.

Animals of an
East African Savanna

Cheetah: 4, 5 Just like the spots and stripes on many predators, a cheetah's spots help it hide in shadows.

Elephant: 6–12 Even elephants can conceal themselves. Their rough gray hides allow them to blend in with bare branches of trees.

Giraffe: 13–18 Many people have reported mistaking a giraffe for an old, dead tree. When the tree walked away, they realized it was actually a giraffe.

Hyena: 19, 20 Hyenas are brown and tan spotted to blend in with the dry grasses of the savanna when they hunt.

Leopard: 21, 22 Leopards hunt in the dim light of dusk and dawn. The spots on their coats help them blend in with shadows.

Lion: 23, 24 Lions are sand colored, which helps them hide as they sneak up on their prey.

Olive baboon: 1–3 The olive

baboon is named for the color of its coat, which at a distance is a shade of green-gray and is perfect for hiding in the grasslands of Africa.

Ostrich (adult) 25, 26; (chick) 27–29: If a female ostrich meets a predator and cannot run away or fight because she has chicks, she lies down with her head on the ground and her wings and tail flat. Her dull brown feathers make her look

like a mound of earth. Her chicks copy her.

Thomson's gazelle (adult) 30–33; (fawn) 34: After giving birth, the mother gazelle hides the fawn in the tall grass and returns twice a day to nurse it until it is old enough to join the herd. Fawns have tawny coloring, which helps them stay camouflaged when hiding in open country.

Zebra: 35–40 The stripes on zebras don't make them blend in with their background; they make them blend in with one another. That means lions cannot separate out one zebra from the group and attack it.

Hide-and-Seek in the Deciduous Forest

Can you find 40 animals?

Deciduous Forests

Some forests change with the seasons: spring, summer, autumn, and winter. These are called deciduous forests. In autumn the leaves on the trees change colors. In winter the leaves fall off, and in spring they grow back. The trees and shrubs provide shelter and food for lots of animals. This forest in England is a busy place in spring.

Animals of an English Deciduous Forest

Badger: 1, 2 Badgers come out at night, when their dark markings make them harder to see.

Fallow deer (fawn) 3; (adult male) 4, 5; (adult female) 6: Young deer have spotted coats so they can hide on the sun-dappled forest floor.

Fox: 7, 8 The fox is the smallest member of the dog family. Its brownish-red coat helps it hide in tall grass.

Gray squirrel: 14–16 Gray squirrels have coats the color of tree bark.

Great spotted woodpecker: 9, 10 This woodpecker spends most of its time clinging to tree trunks and branches, often trying to hide on the side away from the observer.

Green woodpecker: 11–13 The green woodpecker blends in with green leaves.

Hedgehog: 17, 18 When hedgehogs are scared, they roll into prickly, brown balls.

Jay: 19, 20 Although they are the most colorful members of the crow

family, European jays are quite difficult to see because they are shy and rarely move away from cover.

Mole: 21 Moles are the color of dirt, where they dig their burrows.

Rabbit (adult) 22–25; (kits) 26–28: Rabbits have brown coats to blend in with the ground.

Stoat: 29 Stoats, or short-tailed weasels, are brown to match the ground.

Wild boar (adult) 30; (piglets) 31–35: Wild boar piglets are born with brown and white stripes to make them difficult to see in the grass or leaf litter.

Woodcock (adult) 36; (chicks) 37–40: Woodcocks nest on the ground in dead leaves. Their splotchy brown and black feathers make them look like piles of leaves.

Hide-and-Seek in the Snow

Can you find 27 animals?

Snow

The Arctic has long, cold winters with lots of snow and short, cool summers. It includes not only the ice cap around the North Pole, but also areas called tundra, where a few plants grow. It has no trees and is mostly flat. Animals that live all year round in the Arctic have to learn how to survive in extremely cold weather.

Animals of the Arctic

Arctic fox: 1 The arctic fox turns white in the winter to blend in with the snow.

Arctic hare: 2 Arctic hares shed their brown summer fur for white fur in the winter.

Arctic tern: 3, 4 Like most arctic birds, these terns are white.

Beluga whale: 5–8 Beluga whales are white, making it easier for them to swim unseen when they are hunting.

Ermine: 9 These animals are also known as short-tailed weasels. They turn white in the winter. In the summer they turn brown and are called stoats.

Harp seal (adult) **10–12;** (pup) **13, 14:** Young harp seals are famous for their snowy white coats. They are born on floating ice, where they must blend in until they are old enough to swim away from predators.

Lemming: 15–17 Lemmings live in burrows beneath the snow.

Orca: 18, 19 These predators, also called killer whales, have dark backs

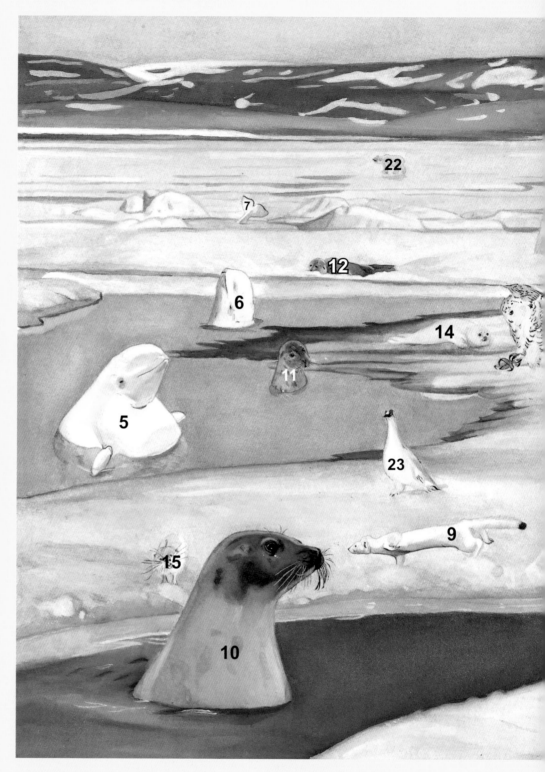

and light bellies. This coloring helps hide them from animals swimming above them because they blend in with the ocean bottom. To animals swimming under them, they blend in with the sky.

Polar bear: 20–22 A polar bear's white fur helps it blend in with the snow and ice.

Ptarmigan: 23 Ptarmigans are seasonally camouflaged; their

feathers change from white in winter to brown in spring or summer.

Snow goose: 24–26 Snow geese are white like snow.

Snowy owl: 27 An adult snowy owl's white feathers make it hard to see against the snow while it hunts lemmings.

Hide-and-Seek on the Coral Reef

Can you find 83 animals?

Coral Reefs

Coral reefs are found in warm, shallow ocean waters. Coral reefs are formed by tiny animals that live in colonies. When these sea creatures die, they leave limestone skeletons. It can take thousands of years for a reef to form. Australia's Great Barrier Reef is the world's largest coral reef.

Animals of the Great Barrier Reef

Blue-ringed octopus: 1 These octopuses can change color to hide.

Blue streak cleaner wrasse: 2 These small fish clean parasites from bigger fish. As a repayment for this service, the bigger fish don't eat them.

Box jellyfish: 3 Jellyfish are clear like glass.

Broadclub cuttlefish: 5 These animals are not really fish, but mollusks related to squids. They can change skin color and pattern to blend in with the background.

Butterfly fish: 6, 7 These fish hide in coral colored like themselves.

Clown fish: 8, 9 Clown fish are not affected by the poisons on the tentacles of sea anemones. They hide among the anemones and may lure other fish that the anemones eat. Like other brightly colored fish, they blend in with the colorful corals.

Coral (brain coral 4, leather coral 67, soft coral 78, staghorn coral 81): Corals come in many different shapes, colors, textures, and sizes. Many fish hide among them.

Coral trout: 10 These fish are named after the coral in which they hide.

Damselfish: 11–15 These vividly colored fish take cover in similarly colored coral.

Fairy basslet: 16–60 These showy fish try to disguise themselves as coral.

False cleaner wrasse: 61 These sneaky fish look like the cleaner wrasse, so they can safely approach larger fish. But instead of cleaning, they bite off fins and scales for food.

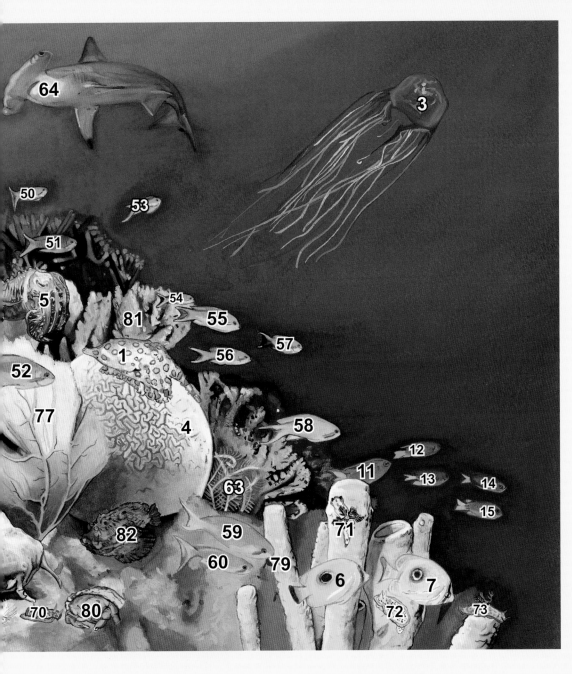

long spines on a lionfish make it hard to tell where the fish begins and ends.

Nudibranch: 69–73 These animals are also called sea slugs. Sometimes they turn the color of the coral they eat.

Sea anemone: 74–76 Sea anemones look like pretty flowers, but they are poisonous. They are predators that eat fish and shellfish but are good places to hide for animals that are not affected by their poison.

Sea fan: 77 Sea fans, like corals, come in many colors. Brightly colored fish and other sea creatures can blend in with them.

Sponge: 79 Many creatures hide among these simple animals that live permanently attached to a location on the bottom.

Sponge crab: 80 The sponge crab hides under a living sponge that it holds on top of its shell with tiny claws on its back legs.

Stonefish: 82 Stonefish are venomous fish that disguise themselves as stones.

Wobbegong shark: 83 The wobbegong shark has sand-colored skin and fleshy tassels on its chin and jaw that look like weeds.

Feather star: 62, 63 Feather stars can range in color from bright yellow to red. They are good places for other animals to hide.

Hammerhead shark: 64 Hammerhead sharks have dark backs and light undersides. To animals swimming above, the sharks blend in with the ocean bottom. To animals swimming below them, they blend in with the sky.

Hawksbill turtle: 65 Patterns on the backs of these turtles look like the ocean floor. Their undersides are light and difficult to see against the sky from below.

Hermit crab: 66 Some hermit crabs attach sea anemones to their shells for camouflage.

Lionfish: 68 The dark stripes and

Index